THE MILITARY OBLIGATION
OF CITIZENSHIP

BY
LEONARD WOOD
Major-General United States Army

PRINCETON UNIVERSITY PRESS
PRINCETON
LONDON: HUMPHREY MILFORD
OXFORD UNIVERSITY PRESS
1915

INTRODUCTION

When General Wood delivered his address in Princeton April 15, 1915, on the subject of "The Policy of the United States in Raising and Maintaining Armies," many of us felt that his words should have a wider circulation; hence this volume.

To the Princeton address have been added two other addresses by General Wood. The first, "The Military Obligation of Citizenship" was delivered at the Lake Mohonk Conference, May 20, 1915. The second, "The Civil Obligation of the Army," was delivered at St. Paul's School, June 15, 1915. These addresses are here reprinted as they appeared in the press.

INTRODUCTION

It is eminently proper that the American people should give especial consideration to the opinion of General Wood on the subject of military preparedness. We should listen to him with particular deference because of his intimate knowledge of our army, its strength and its weakness, and because in the event of war he is the one upon whom would rest the heaviest weight of responsibility to defend our homes against the attack of an invading enemy. General Wood is a soldier, and yet a man of peace. He hates militarism but believes in a reasonable preparedness and naturally shrinks from the task of leading forth the devoted but inexperienced young men of our land to be slaughtered like cattle at the hands of experienced and seasoned troops. He desires to maintain peace with honor, but would not sacrifice honor merely for the sake of a comfortable ease and security of peace. He is deeply sensible of the fact that no amount of patriotic enthusiasm will compensate for the lack of military knowledge, and that in the time of peril the ability to meet the crisis is not born of the crisis itself, but its beginning and development must antedate the occasion when the crucial test is to be met and withstood, and that the easy going and popular idea that when the emergency comes unknown resources will be discovered and extraordinary powers suddenly evoked, is a fallacy as silly as it is false, and that it is disastrous to attempt to learn the art of war in the midst of war itself, because war is the time for action, not for education.

General Wood commands our attention because he himself has done more than merely talk and write on this subject. He has begun the work of general military education through the summer camps, and has attempted with extraordinary success this intensive training of our young men in military theory and practice.

In all the pursuits of professional and business life we have formed the habit of seeking expert knowledge. General Wood possesses this knowledge. It is available in this volume. Our voters and legislators alike should seek the light where it is shining. It does not require an extraordinary amount of wisdom for a man to profit by his own mistakes. It is, however, the supreme test of wisdom and the proof of its presence and power when a man is capable of profiting by the mistakes of others. The same is true not only of the individual, but of any particular generation of people. It is difficult for those who live in the present to understand and profit by the mistakes of the generations before them. That generation is indeed wise that can so interpret the history of the past as to realize the significance of disastrous mistakes due to ignorance and indifference and thereby avoid a like disaster in its own day.

Let us as a nation learn the lesson of our own foolishness so that we may not multiply the mistakes or repeat the folly of those who have gone before us.

JOHN GRIER HIBBEN.

Princeton, N. J.
November 3, 1915

CONTENTS

I. The Policy of the United States in Raising and Maintaining Armies 1

II. The Military Obligation of Citizenship 40

III. The Civil Obligation of the Army 50

I

THE POLICY OF THE UNITED STATES IN RAISING AND MAINTAINING ARMIES

The people of the United States are singularly lacking in information concerning both the military history of their country and its military policy. Students in school and college as a rule receive entirely erroneous ideas on both of these subjects. The average young man, unless he has really made a study of the country's history, is firmly convinced that the Revolutionary War was characterized throughout by the highest quality of patriotism and devotion to the best interests of the country on the part of the people as a whole.

He is not at all familiar with the desperate struggle which was made by Washington, various Colonial assemblies and the Confederation of Colonies, to keep in the field even a small force of troops. He hears very little of the bickerings, mutinies, desertions and frequent changes of personnel which made the war a difficult one to conduct and served to bring out into strong relief the remarkable qualities of Washington—those qualities of patience, good judgment, discretion and again patience, and more patience, which made it possible for him to hold the illy-equipped, disjointed and discordant elements together, and to have always available some kind of a fighting force, although seldom an effective one.

We have as a nation neglected the lessons of past wars, and have learned little from the example of the great military nations, and, as Emory Upton truthfully says: "Our general policy has followed closely that of China." Perhaps this statement may be somewhat extreme in all which applies to conditions up to the end of the Civil War, but it is not in any way extreme when applied to conditions which exist today. The great nations with policies to uphold and interests to defend have made what they believe to be adequate military preparation.

The United States has been drifting for years. No real military preparations of an adequate character have been made. Military preparedness means the organization of all the resources of a nation—men, material and money—so that the full power of the nation may be promptly applied and continued at maximum strength for a considerable period of time. War today, when initiated by a country prepared for war, comes with great suddenness, because all preparations have been made in advance; plans have been worked out to the last detail, organization completed and reserve supplies purchased and assembled long in advance and the whole force of the mighty machine can be applied in a very brief period of time at any designated point.

Back of the machine itself is the railroad service, so organized as to be turned over immediately to the military authorities. Back of this come the civil hospitals, the bakeries, and the supply departments of all sorts, each with its responsibility fixed in case of operations within its area, or in case of a demand for supplies in other sections of the theatre of war. The capacity of every ship is known, and plans completed for her use as a troop ship, and when war threatens, the whereabouts of the shipping is closely watched, and ships are assembled quietly to meet any demand which may be required for over-

MAINTAINING ARMIES

sea operations. These are but an outline of what is meant by military preparedness.

Mere numbers of men and undeveloped military resources are of little value. It has been well said that in the sudden onrush of modern war, undeveloped military resources are of no more use than an undeveloped gold mine in Alaska would be in a panic on Wall Street. The comparison is not overdrawn. You must remember, all of you, that this country has never yet engaged in war with a first-class Power prepared for war.

You must remember also that once sea power is lost or held in check an enormous force can be landed on these shores within a month—a force sufficient to go where it will and to hold whatever it desires to hold.

Why have we failed to make adequate preparation? Partly because of ignorance of the true facts concerning our utter unpreparedness, and partly due to a conceit fostered by the average Fourth of July orator and politician, through statements to the effect that we possess peculiar and remarkable military characteristics which make our soldiers trained and efficient without preparation, and as good as equally brave and equally sound men of other countries who have spent years in training. Again there is the curious Anglo-Saxon prejudice against a large standing army and the feeling that it is always a menace to civil liberty.

In our past wars we were not confronted by great nations with highly organized military machines; steam navigation had not appeared; our possible enemies were without standing armies of any size, and lacked entirely that complete military organization which characterizes them today. It took a long time to get troops together and prepare supplies for them, and a considerable period of time to cross the ocean.

Photo by Department of Enlisted Experts
COAST DEFENSE GUN, FORTRESS MONROE, VA.

Our forefathers had more time to prepare. Then, again, they were more familiar with the use of arms; weapons were of a simple type; they could be made quickly, and instruction in their use was a relatively simple matter.

Now highly organized military establishments are the rule among our possible antagonists. Rapid steam transportation in vast amount is available. The arms of war are extremely complicated and costly: it takes a long time to make them and a long time to instruct soldiers in their use. In other words, today everything is in favor of the prepared aggressor and everything against the unready pacific nation.

The blow comes more quickly and with greater force, and it is not possible to provide even a semblance of protection against it unless wise measures have been taken long in advance.

Since the foundation of the Republic, war has existed as follows:

Revolutionary War	7	years
War of 1812-14	2½	years
Mexican War	2	years
Florida War	7	years
Civil War	4	years
War with Spain and Philippine Rebellion	2	years

Not to mention numerous Indian wars and internal disturbances requiring the use of troops.

We have struggled through these wars and have emerged generally successfully, but in none of them has there been any evidence of well-thought-out preparations or the application of a sound military policy. Our people remember only the success and forget entirely the great and unnecessary cost in blood and treasure in which our defective method of conducting these wars resulted. By faulty methods I mean that we have generally conducted war as a confederacy instead of as a nation. We have permitted altogether too much interference by States. Too many officers have been appointed by the Governors of States. New regiments have been raised oftentimes in order that new officers might be appointed and political patronage increased, whereas the old regiments should have been filled up, as they had acquired experience, some traditions and *esprit,* and were much more valuable than new regiments. This is seen in the Civil War in case of the Wisconsin organizations. Wisconsin had the good sense to veteranize her regiments, and the result is seen when one remembers the term "Iron Brigade" applied to a Wisconsin brigade.

Then again we have had frequently the intervention of civilians, either through the activities of the Secretary of War or of the civil arms of the Government. There has been a general lack of a sense of individual responsibility for military service. Reliance on volunteer enlistments has continued, and has been one of the gravest sources of danger to the Republic. The experience of the Revolution should have taught us that it is not safe in a real war to depend upon volunteers. There is an enthusiastic response by a certain proportion of the best element in the early days of war, but this response cannot be counted upon to continue throughout a long war involving severe strains upon the population, nor is it right or just to throw the burden of military service upon a portion of the population. It is a universal obligation and the country will never be secure or safe until it is recognized as such and measures are taken to develop military preparation on a basis of universal military obligation.

To return to the Revolution, in 1774

Photo by Brown Bros., N. Y.

ROOKIES AT PLATTSBURG

MAINTAINING ARMIES 11

Massachusetts Colony assembled a provisional congress, and began preparations for a conflict with Great Britain. It took steps to organize a militia and to appoint officers. The movement was continued through the year 1775, and provision was made that a portion of the militia should be Minute Men—men who would hold themselves ready to respond immediately to call. This was the condition when the fight at Lexington occurred. Men were commissioned as officers largely in accordance with the number of men they raised. It was a most vicious practice, and one which has persisted until recent times. Popular men, regardless of their military qualifications or fitness, were appointed to commands which they were entirely unfitted to exercise.

In May, 1775, the Continental Congress met (this was about three weeks after the battle of Lexington). It assumed immediately the functions of civil government, but being without authority to levy taxes or to raise revenue, it was empowered to emit bills of credit, their redemption being secured by the promise of the twelve Colonies. This limitation upon its financial power almost neutralized its power to create and support armies. The conduct of the Revolutionary War would have been very different had the Continental Congress had the power to employ the entire financial and military resources of the people. This Congress authorized the formation of ten companies of riflemen, and these companies were really the beginning of the Continental Army. They were raised from Pennsylvania, Virginia and Maryland. The term of enlistment was fixed at one year. There was great enthusiasm, and the twelve companies reported within sixty days. As was natural the men composing these companies were among the best. The really best men are those who first rush to the colors.

These riflemen were the nucleus of the army which finally achieved our independence, and maintained a high reputation throughout the war. The term of enlistment, however, was short, and here we encounter one of the great difficulties which confronted Washington and all others throughout the Revolution; namely, the question of short enlistments. Men were barely trained before they left the service to be replaced by others untrained and, of course, unequipped and generally demanding new uniforms and equipment. Shortly after the authorization of these companies of riflemen Congress authorized twenty-six additional regiments to be raised by the different colonies—sixteen by Massachusetts. Blank commissions were sent to Washington. With the arrival of these blank commissions Washington's troubles and difficulties were greatly augmented. A tremendous struggle followed. States attempted to secure an undue proportion for their own contingents.

Washington's letters at this time speak of corruption, lack of patriotism, slow enlistments, and indicate a condition which would have appalled any but one with a stout heart and determined character.

About this time appeared the question of "bounty"—one of the most dangerous and pernicious methods of securing men. Washington was already deeply impressed with the danger of short enlistments and the unreliability of the Militia. He was also alarmed at the general and widespread evil of desertion. Volunteering had already become slow. Washington recommended coercive measures to the General Court of Massachusetts and urged—indeed almost prayed—Congress

MAINTAINING ARMIES 15

to establish enlistments for the war. He already saw clearly that the volunteer system was a failure, that it was full of grave dangers and that the war could not be successfully conducted by untrained men led by inefficient officers.

It was during this year—thanks largely to the efforts of Washington—that the Continental Army reached its maximum strength—the greatest that it had during the struggle. At its maximum it totaled in round numbers 89,000 men, of whom 49,000 were Continentals and 42,000 Militia. Dictatorial powers were given to Washington to raise troops in any of the Colonies, seize supplies and compel acceptance of colonial bills; from all of which it is clearly evident that had we been opposed by a vigorous, well organized enemy our capacity for resistance would have been comparatively slight.

The British campaign was not pushed

with great energy. From the high water mark of 89,000 the Continental Army shrunk year by year. In 1777 the total was 69,000; in 1778 it had dwindled to 51,000, and such was the condition of the difficulty as to enlistments that the enlistment of negro slaves was authorized by Rhode Island—these slaves to become free on enlistment.

Congress recommended to the States the employment of the draft. These conditions grew worse in 1779. Bounties had to be greatly increased and the total maximum force shrunk to 44,000. In 1780 the same general difficulties continued. The proportion of Continentals to Militia had increased. The grand total was about 43,000, of whom a very considerable number were Militia enlisted for short periods. In 1781 (the last year which was characterized by active fighting), the army had dwindled to a total of a little over 29,000 men; mutiny took place among the troops of the Pennsylvania line, and the general condition was chaotic. Had we been confronted by a well organized enemy and a vigorous campaign waged against us, it is not difficult to foresee what the outcome must have been. Bounties had increased enormously, and discipline was poor among the newly raised troops.

No one who has studied carefully the situation during the last two years of the Revolutionary War can fail to appreciate the tremendous value of the aid which was furnished us by France. It was of vital importance and came at a most critical time. The haphazard policy followed throughout the Revolution cost tremendously in life and treasure. Years after the war General Lee (known as Light-Horse Harry Lee) characterized our military policy as follows:

"While I record with delight facts

which maintain our native and national courage, I feel a horror lest demagogues who flourish in a representative system of government (the best when virtue rules, the wit of man can devise) shall avail themselves of the occasional testimony to produce a great result. Convinced as I am that a government is the murderer of its citizens which sends them to the field uninformed and untaught, where they are to meet men of the same age and strength, mechanized by education and discipline for battle, I cannot withhold my denunciation of its wickedness and folly."

Washington's criticism of our military policy was none the less strong. He says:

"Had we formed a permanent army in the beginning, which, by the continuance of the same men in service, had been capable of discipline, we should never have had to retreat with a handful of men across the Delaware in 1776 trembling for the fate

12-INCH COAST DEFENSE GUN AT FORT WRIGHT

MAINTAINING ARMIES 19

of America, which nothing but the infatuation of the enemy could have saved. . . . We should not have been the greatest part of the war inferior to the enemy, indebted for our safety to their inactivity, enduring frequently the mortification of seeing inviting opportunities to ruin them pass unimproved for want of a force which the country was completely able to afford, and of seeing the country ravaged, our towns burnt, the inhabitants plundered, abused, murdered, with impunity from the same cause. . . . There is every reason to believe that the war has been protracted on this account," etc.

The total number of Regulars engaged during the war was 237,731; the total Militia about 164,000—roughly a total of 395,000 troops. Our maximum was in 1776, when we had 89,000, and it dwindled to a little over 29,000 in 1781. In 1776 the British had 20,171, and in 1781 they had

42,000. In other words, Great Britain, sluggishly as she conducted the war, was, nevertheless growing stronger, and had it not been for the invaluable assistance of France, it is not improbable that the war might have gone against us.

Our people soon forgot the lessons of this war, remembering only that we came out of it successfully. The war was rendered unnecessarily long and expensive, both in men and money, by the total lack of experience of our statesmen in military matters. Our efficiency was undermined by short enlistments and the failure to recognize the danger of dependence on Volunteers; also by ignorance of the fact that the bounty cannot be depended upon in a long war and failure to appreciate the fact that troops are reliable only when they are commanded by well trained officers who have at least received reasonable training and discipline.

Shortly after the close of the war the Army was practically disbanded, except Battery F (known as the "Alexander Hamilton Battery"). This battery has continued in our service since the Revolution and is now Battery F of the 4th Artillery.

Little was apparently learned from the Revolution.

There were reorganizations of the Army in 1790, 1791 and 1792, which resulted finally in an army of 5,500 men. The whole policy, however, was rather haphazard. There was no system worthy of the name for increasing the Army, and no reserve of trained officers; in fact, the mistakes of the Revolution had apparently been forgotten.

In 1792 Baron Steuben, who had been of great value to the Colonies as an organizer and instructor of troops, recommended that the Army be organized as a legion, and the Secretary of War (General Knox) was so impressed with the idea that he proposed to apply the same organization to the Militia, dividing it into three bodies, designated as the Advance, Main and Reserve corps—first, the Advance Corps, to consist of men from 18 to 20 years of age, inclusive—second, the Main Corps, consisting of men from 21 to 45 years of age, inclusive—third, all men from 45 to 60 years of age, inclusive. All members of the Advance Corps under 20 were to receive military instruction for 30 days at annual camps.

Other young men of the Advance Corps were required to be present at least ten days of these encampments. The members of the Main Corps were to receive four days' instruction per year.

Here we find many years in advance of its application in Europe the idea of a nation in arms; in other words, an endorse-

Photo by Brown Bros., N. Y.
ARMY MANEUVERS VAN COURTLAND PARK, N. Y.

ment of the policy recommended by Jefferson: namely, that we must classify and train all our male citizens. In fact, as one studies the papers of the early Presidents, it is evident everywhere that they had in mind the "nation in arms" idea when they spoke of "our main reliance being the Militia," the Militia including, as it did, all men between the ages of 18 and 45. It was the clear intent of the founders of the Republic that all our citizens from 18 to 45 should be trained to such an extent as to make them efficient soldiers.

The legionary organization was adopted for the Army itself, but was never extended to the Militia, nor were the classification and training put in operation.

From the small size and rather temporary character of the regular Military establishment, it is plain that the intention was to depend principally upon a trained Militia, and had this idea been put in operation through an effective system of training, we should have been far better prepared for our subsequent wars, and eventually have adopted a sound military policy, characterized by an appreciation of the necessity of training men and preparing reserves of men and material in advance.

From 1792 reorganizations and shake-ups in the Army continued. The year 1805 was signalized by a very important event in our military history; namely, the establishment at West Point, which was done principally on the recommendation of Alexander Hamilton.

In 1812 the Army was increased in view of the coming war with England. At the commencement of this war the Army consisted of 6,744 men. It was increased in June to twenty-five regiments of Infantry, four Artillery, two of Dragoons and one of Riflemen—a total of 36,700.

MAINTAINING ARMIES 25

It was proposed to raise 30,000 Volunteers.

The war with England began on June 18, 1812. The enemy had a relatively small force of regular troops in Canada—about 4,500 effectives. Our standing army was a little less than 7,000 men. The same old haphazard policy which had characterized the conduct of military matters in the Revolution was continued. Officers who could raise men were given commissions. The Governors of some of the States refused to furnish Militia. The difficulties of a confederacy conducting effective military operations were illustrated. Again the Militia demonstrated its entire unreliability. This war, from the standpoint of military inefficiency, was the least creditable of our wars; in fact, taken as a whole, it was highly discreditable to us on land, and while we had many brilliant individual ship actions at sea, at the end of the war our Navy was practically under blockade, and our commerce almost destroyed.

On land, with the exception of a minor victory on the Thames, and a creditable action at Lundy's Lane, where the Regulars covered themselves with glory, and the victory at New Orleans (fought after the war), our military operations cannot be regarded with any degree of satisfaction. In a word, they were discreditable to us. Washington was captured by a force much less in numbers than that of the defenders —with a loss on our side of only eight killed and eleven wounded.

We put into this war 527,000 men. Of this number approximately 33,481 were officers. The largest number of British regular troops which were on the continent at any one time during this war was approximately 16,800. In coöperation with them were some thousands of Militia and

Indians. These, however, constituted a very small force in comparison with the number which we put into the field.

These figures bring out very forcibly the necessity of training a large body of officers in advance of war. Especially is this important if we are to depend in any way upon Volunteers.

The lessons of the war are so clear that it seems hardly necessary to state that it was a repetition in the gravest form of many of the blunders of the Revolution, which had only too often their origin in defective military legislation and lack of preparation, making it possible, as Upton puts it, that "less than 5,000 men for a period of two years brought war and devastation into our territory and successfully withstood the misapplied power of seven millions of people."

Shortly after the war the Army was reduced to 10,000. In 1817 came the Seminole War and the same haphazard policy through enlistments of many different men. New arms, new equipments, waste of money and waste of life—the same policy runs through the Indian wars in which we were engaged in subsequent years.

During the Seminole and Creek Wars relatively enormous forces of troops were employed in comparison with the small force of Indians who opposed us. The cost in blood, life and treasure was unnecessarily great. The whole conduct of the war spelt poor organization and lack of intelligent military policy.

In 1838 the Army was increased to about 12,500. In 1842 it was again reduced to 8,600. In 1846 the rumble of the approaching Mexican war was heard, and there was a gradual increase in the Army. During that war it was increased to about 39,000 Regulars. At the end of the war it was again reduced to 10,300. There was a serious effort made during this war to increase the enlistment period and to fix it at a minimum of twelve months, or for the war. The total number of men employed during this war was 104,000. It was a brilliantly successful war, and to quote again from Upton, who is almost the sole authority from which we draw accurate data concerning our wars:

"Successes so brilliant would apparently denote the perfection of military policy, but, paradoxical as it may seem, official documents establish the fact that they were achieved under the very same system of laws and executive orders which in the preceding foreign war had led to a series of disasters culminating in the capture and destruction of our capital.

"The explanation of this paradox is to be found partly in the difference of character of our adversaries, but more especially in the quality of the Regular Army, with which we began the two wars. For the Mexican War, as for the War of 1812, the Government had ample time to prepare."

This quotation covers the situation very well. Our enemy was not a well prepared enemy, and the scene of action was so distant from the source from which troops were drawn that the troops were in hand for a long enough period to get them into fairly effective shape. There was an exceptionally efficient body of regular officers.

Again there was a relatively small force of militia employed—only 12,500 out of a force of 104,000 as compared with 458,000 out of a force of 521,000 in the War of 1812.

We now come to the great Civil War. Our population was nearly 31,000,000. We had a small regular army scattered over a vast area. It numbered a little over 16,000 men. Some of it was west of the Mississippi; in fact, it was scattered from the Canadian border to the Mexican frontier, and drawn out in a thin line along our western frontier. We were unprepared as usual. Fortunately the seceding States were equally unprepared, and it was a case of two nations entering into war, both unprepared, and each having to develop its military resources in the way of men and material as the war went on. There is no doubt whatever in the mind of any intelligent student of military matters that had either side possessed a well organized and well disciplined force of 50,000 men, that that side would have occupied the other's capital almost immediately.

Dependence was placed upon both Militia and Volunteers. The Militia was unsatisfactory, as has generally been the case. The conduct of Governors was too often characterized by party affiliations. The political aspects of the war are too well known to require discussion.

The main dependence of the country was placed upon the Volunteers. This was true of both North and South, and in each instance it was necessary to go to the draft. The cost in blood and treasure was tremendous. Out of this military chaos eventually came two splendid armies—armies, however, created at tremendous cost.

The old policy was adopted—first Militia and Volunteers, followed by the draft, bounties with their attendant evils, widespread desertion, bounty jumping, etc. Fortunately it was a struggle amongst ourselves. Had the country as a whole been attacked by a well organized nation of equal population, but with fully developed military resources, we could have looked for but one result. The lessons of all the above referred to wars point out very clearly to what our weakness has been due, namely, first—the lack of any adequate military preparation, second—dependence upon an unsound military policy, as indicated by the maintenance of an inadequate Regular Army and dependence upon Militia and Volunteers; also failure to avail ourselves of the full military strength of the nation.

Again quoting Upton: "Any Government which foregoes its rights to compulsory military service becomes more and more enslaved by depending solely upon voluntary military service, induced by gifts of money, land and clothing."

The voluntary system failed us in the past, and will fail us in the future. It is uncertain in operation, prevents organized preparation, tends to destroy that individual sense of obligation for military service which should be found in every citizen, costs excessively in life and treasure, and does not permit that condition of preparedness which must exist if we are to wage war successfully with any great power prepared for war. The question is: What shall we do to adequately prepare ourselves for war, without establishing a huge standing army or bringing about a condition which might be described as one of militarism, which term, as I use it, means the condition under which the military forces of a nation demand and secure special recognition, both socially and officially, and exercise an undue influence in the conduct of the civil affairs of the government, both at home and abroad. In other words, a condition which may be described as one under which the military element dominates the nation's policy. Nothing could be more unfortunate than the establishment of such a condition in this country or elsewhere, so far as development on normal lines is concerned.

However, a condition of thorough preparedness can be established without creating a condition of militarism. Switzerland is an illustration of this possibility. Here we have a country noted for its patriotism, distinguished for conservatism and good government, with a people noted for intelligence, industry and good conduct, yet every man who is physically fit has, with few exceptions, received a sufficient amount of military training to fit him to be an efficient soldier.

It has been accomplished in great part during his school period, and at camps of instruction during his youth, and so thorough and complete is the system that at the end of his school and other training received during this period it is only necessary to give him from two to three months intensive training in camp, according to the arm in which he is to serve, to fit him for the final discharge of his duties. The training for officers is, of course, extended over longer periods, but all of this training is accomplished without any interference worthy of consideration with the youth's educational and industrial career. In fact, he is better physically, morally and better as a citizen, because of his training. He has learned to respect the flag of his country and to have a proper regard for the rights of others, and he has had built up in him an appreciation of his obligation to serve the country in time of war. He realizes that this is a tax on which all others depend, and on the payment of which in good faith the life of the nation itself rests.

Australia has inaugurated a somewhat similar system, having in view the same general purpose; namely, the preparation of every male who is physically fit for military duty. Our situation, of course, differs from that of Switzerland, because we must maintain at all times a standing army adequate for the peace needs of the nation. By this I mean the garrison of the Panama Canal, Alaska and the oversea possessions; also a force within continental United States adequate to meet the needs of the country in the way of furnishing garrisons for the sea coast defenses and a sufficient mobile force to control internal disorders or to provide an expeditionary force for minor operations, such as those incident to the recent occupation of Cuba or Vera Cruz.

The Swiss system costs about $6,500,000 a year. There can be no question of its benefit to the people from an economic standpoint, as well as from a military standpoint. The influence in bettering citizenship is shown in the criminal rate of Switzerland, which is only a small fraction of our own. We must adopt a system based on these general lines if we are ever to be efficiently prepared for war or, better said, prepared against war, for our preparation is really an insurance against war rather than an incentive to it. Do not place any dependence upon the statements of these charlatans who speak of a million men flocking to arms between sun and sun, but remember when you hear fallacies of this sort the words of old Light-Horse Harry Lee, which are as true today as they were when they were uttered. We must preserve our ideals, strive for world peace, and do what we can to build up the adjustment of international difficulties through arbitration, but we must not fail to give due heed to the conditions under which we live. Whatever we may hope for in the way of universal peace does not justify us in disregarding the conditions which surround us today. If we want to hand down to our children the heritage which has come to us from our fathers, we must not place confidence in idle boasting

Coast Defense Gun, Fort Hamilton, N. Y.

MAINTAINING ARMIES

but give serious heed to well thought out preparation and adopt a policy for the future with reference to our military establishment very different from that which has existed in the past. We can do this without violating our ideals. If I were to state such a military policy I would say, briefly, have an Army sufficient for the peace needs of the nation, a good Militia, an adequate Navy, and behind them the largest possible number of men trained to be efficient soldiers if needed, but in time of peace following their ordinary civil occupations—ready to come when wanted. A country so prepared will have the largest possible measure of peace.

II

THE MILITARY OBLIGATION OF CITIZENSHIP

I always have impressed upon me at meetings of this kind the evident failure on the part of members of the conference to appreciate the position of officers of the Army and Navy with reference to the military situation. The officers of the Army and Navy are the professional servants of the Government in matters pertaining to the military establishment, and its agents in the conduct of military operations when such become necessary. They do not initiate wars. You are mostly business men engaged in trade and commerce. Nine-tenths of all wars have their origin directly or indirectly in issues arising out of trade. You the people make war; the Government declares it; and we, the officers of the Army and Navy, are charged with the responsibility of terminating it with such means and implements as you may give us.

Being more or less familiar with the requirements of the military situation, we naturally try to impress upon you the necessity of a reasonable degree of preparedness, both in the way of personnel, proper organization and material resources. We realize far more fully than you how necessary organized preparation is, especially in these days when our possible opponents are so thoroughly equipped and entirely ready for military activity.

There is a tendency at all these conferences to invoke the advice of Washington, Jefferson, Adams and other of our presidents and statesmen, given in the past to our countrymen on many matters, but I have heard no reference this year or last as to their advice on the question of military preparedness. You all, of course, know how earnestly Washington, Jefferson, Adams and many others urged upon our people the vital importance of preparedness as the best means of preventing war. Washington frequently urges this upon the attention of our people, as does Jefferson in messages and in his letters to Monroe. Adams states it tersely to the effect that it is the only means by which we can preserve peace. The soundness and correctness of this advice is apparent to all soldiers and it has been again and again brought to the attention of our people. Light-Horse Harry Lee, of the Revolution, said:

"Convinced as I am that a government is the murderer of its citizens which sends them to the field uninformed and untaught, where they are to meet men of the same age and strength, mechanized by education and discipline for battle, I cannot withhold my denunciation of its wickedness and folly."

Those words were absolutely true at the time they were uttered and they are equally true today, and I want to impress upon you who know so little of war, that those of us whose business it is to know something of it and the requirements in the way of preparation, are most deeply concerned, not only from the standpoint of military efficiency, but also on the broad general grounds of common humanity, in establishing a system under which our young men may receive that degree of training which will better fit them to discharge with a reasonable degree of efficiency their duties as soldiers in the defence of the country in case they are needed and thereby tend to reduce to the lowest possible terms the cost in blood and treasure and to make such expenditure as is inevitable, efficient and of value, instead of wasting precious lives without avail. Our President in his last message states:

"It will be right enough, right American policy, based upon our accustomed principles and practices, to provide a system by which every citizen who will volunteer for the training may be made familiar with the use of modern arms, the rudiments of drill and maneuver, and the maintenance and sanitation of camps."

There are several things which have rendered preparedness necessary to a greater extent than ever before; the first is the great improvement in transportation. In the days when Washington, Jefferson and Adams were urging upon us the necessity of preparedness, our possible enemies were without anything like the military establishment of the great powers of today. Transportation over the sea was by sailing ship, and was slow and very difficult, and consequently considerable time was given for preparation. Indeed, there is no department connected with military preparedness in which there has been a greater advance than in means of transportation. There has also been a great advance made in the power and efficiency of weapons. They have become more complex, many of them are very intricate machines which require a great degree of skill in their handling, with resulting long period of instruction on the part of the personnel. The advance in weapons is quite as notable as that in transportation, and the weapon of today is as far ahead of the weapon in the times of Washington as is the vestibule train ahead of the cart of those days. In other words on one side we have a greatly increased condition of preparedness and greatly shortened period of approach through betterment in the means of transportation, and on the other hand we have consequently a shortened period to get ready combined with the necessity of familiarizing ourselves not with the simple weapons of our fathers but with the complex and intricate weapons of today requiring a high degree of skill in their use; the unprepared, unready defense labors under greater embarrassments than ever and the prepared aggressor has more in his favor than ever before.

The officers of the Army and Navy are as I have said not the persons who make wars, their task is to conduct them as efficiently as possible, and by efficiently I mean not only efficiency in the ordinary sense of the term but efficiency in all which pertains to the saving of life. We do not want to see the youth of this country sent to arms untrained and unready to meet equally good men who are trained and ready and while we may all earnestly hope that war will be no more, we are convinced that for the present at least such is not the case. We must judge the future largely by the past and however earnestly we may hope to avoid war there is nothing in the history of the past or the events of the present or the promises of the future which justifies the assumption that we shall not be again confronted by war, and those of us who know what war means want you to approve those moderate, reasonable and necessary measures which will tend in the first place to prevent war, and in case it is unavoidable will tend to make it as short and as little costly in blood and treasure as possible.

If you were living under conditions which rendered it necessary for your boys and men to furnish the crews for the life boat service you would see to it that they knew how to row and swim so that they would be prepared for the dangers of the work which you knew would some day come to them and if any one pressed untrained boys into such service you would say that it was little short of murder. This is what Light-Horse Harry Lee said with reference to the untrained troops of the Revolution, and it is what those of us who know something of war and of the necessary preparation therefor say will be the case if the youth of this country are again sent into war unprepared to efficiently discharge their duties. We are working not for war, but for preparation in the first place against it and in the second place for preparation which if it comes will render it as short and bloodless as possible. While cherishing our ideals and hopes for the future and continuing our efforts to bring about desired results in the way of world peace, we must not be misled or unmindful of the actual conditions which surround us today and will surround us for an indefinite period of time; in other words, we can not without jeopardizing the best interests of our country fail to make proper preparations against possible war; such preparations will exert the largest measure of influence for peace, and in case war is forced upon us, will enable us to conduct it with the least possible expenditure of blood and treasure.

III

THE CIVIL OBLIGATION OF THE ARMY

It is always an inspiration to meet a body of enthusiastic youngsters who have the world ahead of them, and if one can do anything to make more clear the responsibilities and obligations which confront them and suggest a way to meet and overcome them, it is a duty which should be performed. What I wish to say to you may sound a bit harsh and inject an element of seriousness into this occasion which will tend a little to take from it the spirit of joyousness. I am going to say something to you about your obligations to the country as soldiers, for you come of the stock and represent a class whose responsibility to the country in time of war has always been generous.

I noticed today your fine soldiers' monument, erected in honor of the graduates of the school who gave their lives in the nation's service in the Spanish War. Among them are the names of men of my regiment. The response of these men is indicative of the response which is going to be made by men of their kind in the future. You are going to respond whether you are trained or not. What I want to bring home to you is that to be a really good citizen of a republic which is dependent upon its citizen army you must be not only willing but prepared, and I want to say to the parents and friends assembled here tonight that they must remember that these youngsters are going to respond to the call of the country whether they wish it or not; that it is a duty which the great majority of right minded boys will not attempt to shirk, and the question I want to ask them is—Are they going to send these boys to us prepared to be efficient soldiers or are they going to send them to us untrained and unprepared to make such sacrifice as they may have to make effective?

This subject was brought home to me very forcibly the other day by a letter received from a friend in the West, who had just lost his boy in the battle at Ypres. He said:

"You remember the last time we met that I told you of my 17-year-old boy at school in England. Well, he left school and went into the Home Defense force, but this was not enough, and he transferred and joined a regiment at the front —one of the new regiments—and was killed at Ypres. It was sad enough and hard enough to lose the boy, but I shall never be able to get rid of the feeling that neither he nor his mates had a sporting chance; they were unprepared and untrained."

Before going into the details of this subject I want to impress one fact upon you, and that is that our country has never yet in its entire history met single handed a first-class country prepared for war. The shrinkage in enlistments and steady diminution in the strength of our military establishment during our struggle for independence points out clearly and conclusively to any fair-minded person the invaluable assistance of France in the Revolution. In the War of 1812-1814 we were, from a military standpoint, a minor issue, for Great Britain was engaged in that tremendous struggle with Napoleon —a struggle which required the great bulk of her forces on sea and land and prohibited her from concentrating her efforts upon the war in America.

The question is—Shall we drift on, regardless of the teachings of history, making no adequate preparation for the possibilities of the hour, or shall we take heed from the experiences of the past, not only of our own country, but of all lands since history was written, which is, that preparedness is the best insurance against war, or shall we accept as our guide for the future the theory of those deluded people who tell us that wars are over and that this is the last great war, forgetful of the fact that these same people, or people of the same type of intelligence, announced that the Russo-Japanese War was the last war, then that the Balkan War was the last war? The answer is no. We must judge the future by the past and make wise preparation to protect and safeguard those rights which our forefathers handed down to us. It seems to me that no right-minded person can hesitate in deciding

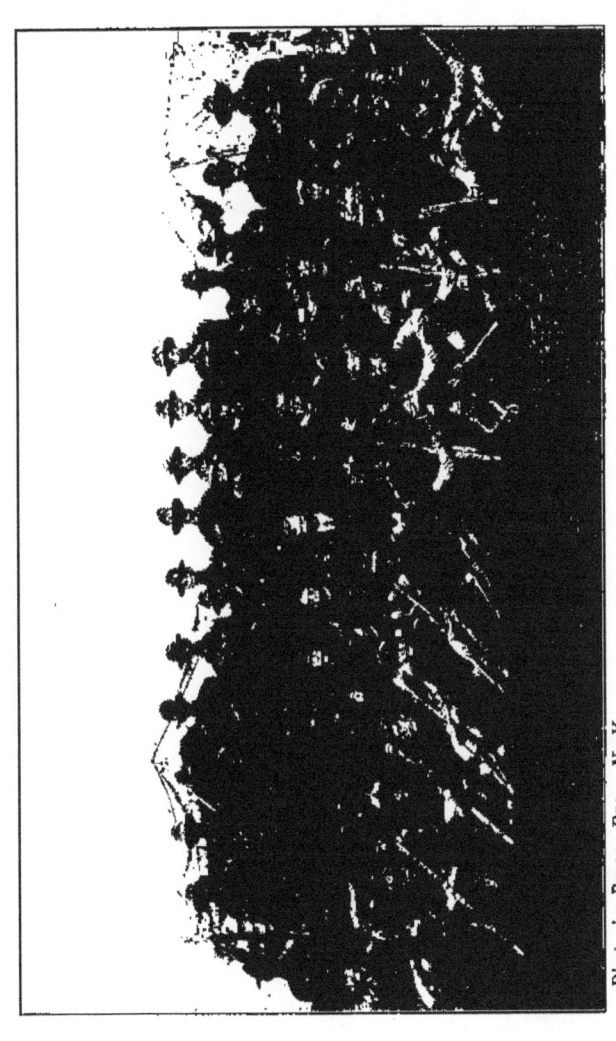

Photo by *Brown Bros., N. Y.*

PRINCETON STUDENTS AT MILITARY CAMP, PLATTSBURG, N. Y.

which is the path of wisdom and which is the path of folly.

We do not want war, but we must not forget that there is many a peace which is infinitely worse than war, such as a peace which results from failure to do our clear duty to fight for what we believe is right or to support our honest convictions. We in this country do not want a large standing army, nor do we desire anything which savors of militarism. We do need and those who are intelligent enough to appreciate the situation want, an adequate army. By this I mean an army sufficient for the peace needs of the nation, which means the garrisoning of the Philippines, Panama, Hawaii, Alaska and Porto Rico, together with such force in the United States as will be sufficient for an expeditionary force, such as we sent to Cuba, or to deal with internal disorders which neither the police nor militia may be adequate to control.

We must have an adequate navy, sufficient to perform a navy's function—on one ocean in any case, and, if we are wise, on both oceans. Both the army and navy must be supported by adequate reserves—the navy with a reserve strong enough to completely man the second line ships ordinarily out of commission and the many supply ships and auxiliary ships which must be put into commission in time of war, and in addition men enough to make good the losses of the first six months of war. We must also have a good Militia with reserves, under a large measure of federal control—a Militia whose response to the calls of the nation will be prompt and certain—one which will come well trained and well equipped. This can only be accomplished through the Federal Government fixing the standards and exercising the necessary power of inspection. Unless this can be done the Militia cannot be considered a dependable force. Back of it is that great force of citizen soldiers, ordinarily known as volunteers—a force which must be trained in time of peace, in order to be promptly available in time of war. In any case the officers of this force must be provided in time of peace and their provision must include thorough, systematic training.

We cannot depend upon volunteers in future wars, as we have in past wars, for the simple reason that the onrush of a modern war is so sudden and all our possible antagonists, concerning whom we need have any serious apprehension, are so thoroughly prepared that there will be no time to train volunteers, and certainly no time to train officers. Washington and the officers of his time were convinced of the folly of depending upon volunteers. They come with a rush from the best of the population during the early stages of war, but their enthusiasm soon passes away and the bounty and the draft follow. In the Revolution our greatest force was, in 1776, about 89,000 men. It dwindled year by year so that in 1781 we had in the field only a little over 29,000 men, and this notwithstanding large bounties of money and land and the strongest efforts on the part of individuals and Colonial assemblies. The same thing took place in the War of 1812-1814. Men came for a short time, but new men had to take their places; 527,000 different men were in the field during this war. Of this number something over 33,000 were officers.

The frequent change of personnel resulted in demoralization and inefficiency. It was again attempted through the bounty to produce effects which should have been produced by patriotism. In the Revolution, which was really the birth struggle of the nation, the falling off in

OF THE ARMY 59

volunteering is worthy of the most serious consideration, as is the chaotic condition which resulted from the working of the same system in the War of 1812-1814. This war on land was highly discreditable to us. With the exception of a drawn battle at Lundy's Lane and an unimportant victory on the Thames, our land operations were not only disastrous, but generally highly discreditable. We abandoned Washington to a force of only about six per cent of that of the defenders, with a loss on our side of eight killed and eleven wounded. The greatest force of regulars which England had in this country at any time during the war was a little over 16,800. There was, of course, a considerable number of Indians and Militia, but this combined force was only a small fraction of our numerically great force. At the battle of New Orleans (fought after the war) we won a highly creditable victory. Our troops were well handled and the enemy attempted the impossible. Moreover, the bulk of the men who composed Jackson's army were expert with the rifle.

On the water we had many highly creditable individual ship actions and some creditable fleet actions, but generally speaking, on the high seas our commerce was destroyed and our gallant but small navy bottled up.

In the Civil War we of necessity continued the volunteer system, no general policy looking to military efficiency having been inaugurated, and the two armies, each undisciplined and untrained, learned the game of war together, and after several years were moulded into excellent fighting machines. In this war, as in preceding wars, the volunteer system failed absolutely, and both the North and the South had to go to the draft and every attendant evil of the bounty system, with its accompanying desertions, bounty jumping, etc., which tended to demoralize the public conscience in all which pertained to the sacredness of the military obligation. The number of desertions was enormous. Charles Francis Adams places it as high as 523,000 out of a total enlistment in the northern armies of something over 2,700,-000, or nearly one in five.

In the Mexican War we met an unprepared and rather ineffective enemy and the theater of war was so remote that our men were in hand long enough to get them into reasonably good shape, at least to meet an enemy of the type which confronted us. We had, moreover, an unusually able body of officers, many of whom distinguished themselves greatly in the Civil War; but again, as in all our wars, had we met a prepared and efficient enemy the system would have been our undoing.

You must never for a moment accept the very common idea, brought into being largely by the politicians and the Fourth of July orator, that we as a nation have peculiar military ability and that without thorough training we can meet equally good men who have been well trained.

The cowardly abandonment of our capital almost without loss on our part shows how unsafe it is to trust untrained troops in combat with well-organized, well-disciplined troops. You must remember also that this particular action occurred almost within a generation of the Revolutionary War, and that the men who made up the force defending Washington were drawn from sections which produced many of the best troops of the Revolution. Old Light-Horse Harry Lee summed the situation as follows:

"That government is a murderer of its citizens which sends them to the field uninformed and untaught, where they are to meet men of the same age and strength, mechanized by education and discipline for battle."

Those words are just as true and just as applicable today as they were when they were uttered. We are no longer an Anglo-Saxon race, but a very mixed one. Blood strains from all parts of Europe run through out people, and their influence is felt in the descendants of the new-comers. Everything indicates the necessity today, more than ever before, of thorough preparation. Now, while we do not desire a large standing army, we must have the kind of army and an army of the strength referred to above. We must have also a great body of 35,000 or 40,000 reserve officers trained and ready to serve as officers of volunteers. We must have a sound military system—one which tends to produce in the heart of every boy the consciousness of the fact that he is one of the defenders of the country and impels him to make the necessary preparation.

The military systems of Switzerland or Australia appeal to me very strongly as models which we could follow to our advantage in all which pertains to military training. Switzerland has had her system in operation long enough to make its application general, and as a result, while a peaceful, orderly country, she stands always ready to defend her rights and to guard her territory. She is absolutely free from all indication of militarism, as ordinarily understood, and yet every man in Switzerland who is physically fit has received a sufficient amount of training to make him an effective and efficient soldier; that this has served to benefit and uplift the people is conclusively shown by her low criminal rate, which is only a fraction of ours, and by the admitted conservatism of her people, their law-abiding habits, their patriotism and their respect for the rights of others. Contrast her position of today with that of another small European country, which, unlike her, had not made due preparation. In both Switzerland and Australia a large amount of instruction is given through public schools or during the school period of the youth—so much, indeed, that only two or three months of intensive training in camp are necessary to complete the training of the soldier. The officers take a longer and more intensive course, but the system in both countries is worked out so that there is practically no interference with the industrial or educational careers of those under training.

As I have said before, there has been little or no interest in this country in this great question of military training. There has been a general haphazard policy and a blind dependence upon volunteers; in other words, a dependence upon someone else doing one's work. It is an illogical system. There is no reason why one group of the population should assume that another group is going to voluntarily perform their military duties. The obligation to military service is universal. It is a tax upon which all others depend, and a nation which fails to recognize this prepares its own downfall. This general training can all be effected as has been done in Switzerland and Australia, without a trace of militarism, without any departure from ideals, and with a great resulting improvement in the morals, physique and character of our youth. In Switzerland and Australia the training of young boys is principally of a calisthenic character. Later they pass to rifle shooting and military formations. The final finish is put upon them in training at the camps which immediately precede their

OF THE ARMY 67

entry into the first line of the country's defense.

You must not think that war is one of the great destroyers of human life. It does take many lives, but it is among the lesser causes of loss of life. Our industrial casualties, not deaths necessarily, but casualties of all kinds, amount to something over 450,000 a year. Of these, about 78,000 or 79,000 result fatally—a loss rather exceeding the average loss of life of two years of the Civil War. Most of these accidents are preventable. The public interest in life saving is not sufficiently keen to insist on adequate legislation to this end. The losses in the war are more dramatic, more startling, but the lives lost in every day work in the struggle for existence exceed them vastly in number and run on without ceasing, both during peace and war.

The following is a little illustration of

the case of our own country, namely, in ten peaceful Fourths of July (the last July 4, 1910), approximately 1,800 persons were killed and something over 35,000 wounded in celebrating the success of a war which ended nearly 130 years before. The number killed equals the number killed in battle or who died of wounds in the Spanish-American War, the Philippine rebellion and the Indian wars of a number of years preceding. The wounded of these ten peaceful days aggregate seven and a half times the wounded of all these wars. I tell you these things not to prove that war is any less dreadful, or that you should strive less to avoid it, but simply to present to you the truth with reference to the causes which bring about loss of life. Do not give up your ideals. Strive for universal peace, but while striving do not forget the conditions under which you are living, and, however much you may hope to obtain a condition of world peace, remember that there is no evidence of it today and that if we want to preserve the institutions which have been handed down to us we must be ready to defend them or, as Lord Roberts said:

"Strive to stir up, to foster and develop the manly and more patriotic spirit in the nation—a spirit which will induce our youth to realize that they must be not only ready but prepared to guard the heritage handed down to them."

Abandon the theory of chance and adopt that of probability in making wise provisions for peace through preparedness for war.

You hear a great deal about the destructive work of the soldier. I am going to say just a word with reference to his constructive and life saving work, which has really been his principal function since the close of the Spanish-American War, and indeed it was one of his principal activities during that war. Starting with Porto Rico, we find that, principally due to the efforts of a medical officer of the army, Dr. Bailey K. Ashford, tropical anemia, or hookworm disease, as it is ordinarily called, has been about eliminated. Not only was this discovery of value in Porto Rico, but it was made use of throughout our own southern states, with a result of revitalizing and reënergizing hundreds of thousands of people afflicted with this disease. The annual death rate in Porto Rico alone was reduced by a number exceeding the total number of men killed during the Spanish-American War, and a recent inquiry made of all planters in the island with reference to their workers indicates that, in their opinion, the average increase in efficiency is 60 per cent—a truly startling figure, and one which illustrates very well the far-reaching and wonderful effects

WEST POINT CADETS IN TARGET PRACTICE

of sanitary measures and preventative medicine.

Passing on to Cuba, here we have the wonderful discovery of Major Walter Reed and his associates, Carroll and Lezear, which resulted in discovering the method of transmission of yellow fever and the means of controlling it, and the eventual elimination of that dread disease not only from Cuba, but from all the American troops, with the resulting saving in life, which runs into many thousands each year, and a saving in money so vast that it is difficult to estimate it; for the days of yellow fever, with the consequent quarantine, which tied up the movement of men and materials throughout the entire South, limited the movements of ships coming from yellow fever countries, and the costly disinfection, resulted in an expenditure running into hundreds of millions. Indeed, it is safe to say that the saving from yellow fever alone every year in life and money has exceeded the cost in each of the Spanish-American War and the Philippine rebellion.

In the Philippines splendid sanitary work has been done by the army and later by the civil government. Berri berri, one of the most dreaded of the eastern diseases, has been done away with. Malaria has been brought under control. Infant mortality has been halved. Most of this latter work has been done under the civil government, but the foundations were laid by the medical officers of the army who at first had charge of the work. In Panama we see the direct effect of this work in the completion of the Panama Canal. This great and splendid piece of engineering, remarkable as it is from an engineering standpoint, and conducted with wonderful efficiency by General Goethals and his assistants, could not have been built had it not been for the application by General Gorgas of the results of the sanitary discoveries made in Cuba which made it possible to carry on this great work under conditions of health which equalled those anywhere in the United States. It may be truly said without taking one atom of credit from the engineers that this great work was built on a sanitary foundation. Had we not got rid of yellow fever and learned to control malaria, the death rate would have been so heavy that the work could only have resulted in our hands as it did in the hands of the French, for nothing demoralizes working forces more effectively than great epidemics. They are worse than battles in some ways.

The mobilization on the Mexican frontier has not been without its great and lasting benefits. It enabled us, because of the prevalence of typhoid in the Mexican villages and along the Rio Grande, to insist upon general typhoid inoculation of officers and men, and the result has been the removal of typhoid from the army. Last year there were 100,000 men scattered from Tientsin to Panama, through the Hawaiian Islands and the Philippines, from Alaska to Porto Rico, as well as all over the United States, and there was not a single death among them from typhoid. When one remembers thousands of cases in the camps of the Spanish-American War, the importance of this discovery is appreciated. The general application was made possible only by the mobilization of troops and in the struggle to protect them. So it was with the discovery concerning yellow fever and the elaboration of the methods employed in controlling malaria. The results of these discoveries are now all of general application, not only to the population in our own country, but to the population of all countries in and bordering on the American tropics, as well as in the insular possessions. Not only were great sanitary results secured through the military arms of the government, but it should be remembered also that it, the military arm, established and maintained a civil government in Porto Rico, Cuba and the Philippines, and conducted these governments with great success—in Cuba up to the point of the transfer to the Cuban people of a completely organized republic, and in Porto Rico until the transfer to the American civil government; likewise in the Philippines the military authorities were in full charge during the most trying period and turned over to the civil commission which followed them a well-organized government and a well-filled treasury.

I tell you all this in order that you may understand more fully what the real work of the army has been—that its life saving has counterbalanced scores of times its work as a destructive force, if one may apply the term "destructive forces" to a force used to terminate intolerable conditions and to establish humane, just and equitable governments among dependent people.

www.ingramcontent.com/pod-product-compliance
Lightning Source LLC
Chambersburg PA
CBHW032130090426
42743CB00007B/550